A Memory of Manaus

Wonderfully cosmopolitan poems by a poet who seems to have gone everywhere and noticed everything. And read everything, too. Exotic locales in Manaus, Oman, and Kochi—by way of Paris and London—are balanced by imaginative settings in Niagara Falls, Taos, and Cripple Creek. A sensitive, nuanced Baedeker for the mind.

—Jared Carter, Poet

Perhaps the most astonishing aspect of Catharine Brosman's new book is its unflagging inventiveness of both idea and form. After so many poems published, this volume still is full of unexpected delights. This poet's metrical flexibility, power of observation, and resources of imagination never disappoint.

—R.V. Young, Professor Emeritus of English,
North Carolina State University and former Editor, *Modern Age*

A Memory of Manaus exhibits technical mastery and offers a defense of traditional literary theory and humanistic thought. It contains several illuminating translations of Baudelaire and ends with an ekphrastic sequence of eight short pieces on different saints composed in classically sculpted stanzas and rhymed verse. Typical of Brosman's poetry, we find a highly developed sense of place with brilliant evocations of nature (rivers, deserts, plants, fruits, animals, ancient stones). We wander with the poet as she forages through back roads and inlets in the bayous of Louisiana, in several different *paysages* in France, all laden with memories, to the heart of Amazonia, as the title suggests.

As always, Brosman travels with her literary companions—Mallarmé, Saint-Exupéry, Malraux, Sartre, Swift, Dickens—who appear intermittently. Here, however, it is Albert Camus whose presence silently makes itself felt throughout the volume. We experience the poet's "sense of exile" as she savors our earthly kingdom with her husband, Pat. The fates are everywhere present, "reweaving patterns on their loom," as these two traveling lovers in their eighties ("preserved together by some prescient star") move from place to place. We sense Brosman's constant fear that Pat will take yet another crippling fall. Stiff and weary, they make their way where "Life dangles by a thread." To do so, the poet becomes like one of her personages, "a skilled funambulist," leading her husband precariously "along the Old Age River trail."

—Patrick Henry, Cushing Eells Emeritus Professor of Philosophy
and Literature, Whitman College, Walla Walla, Washington

MERCER UNIVERSITY

MERCER UNIVERSITY PRESS

Endowed by

TOM WATSON BROWN

and

THE WATSON-BROWN FOUNDATION, INC.

A Memory of Manaus

Poems

CATHARINE SAVAGE BROSMAN

MERCER UNIVERSITY PRESS
MACON, GEORGIA
2017

MUP/ P551

© 2017 by Mercer University Press
Published by Mercer University Press
1501 Mercer University Drive
Macon, Georgia 31207

9 8 7 6 5 4 3 2 1

Books published by Mercer University Press are printed on acid-free paper
that meets the requirements of the American National Standard for
Information Sciences—Permanence of Paper for Printed Library Materials.

ISBN   978-0-88146-630-0
Cataloging-in-Publication Data is available from the Library of Congress

To my husband, my daughter,
and her family,
with love, always;
and in memory of my parents

"No people can live without beauty."
—Albert Camus, *Carnets*

Also by Catharine Savage Brosman

POETRY
Watering (1972)
Abiding Winter (1983) [chapbook]
Journeying from Canyon de Chelly (1990)
Passages (1996)
The Swimmer and Other Poems (2000) [chapbook].
Places in Mind (2000)
Petroglyphs: Poems and Prose (2003) [chapbook].
The Muscled Truce (2003)
Range of Light (2007)
Breakwater (2009)
Trees in a Park (2010) [chapbook]
Under the Pergola (2011)
On the North Slope (2012)
On the Old Plaza (2014)

CREATIVE PROSE
The Shimmering Maya and Other Essays (1994)
Finding Higher Ground: A Life of Travels (2003)
Music from the Lake and Other Essays (2017)

CRITICISM
André Gide: l'évolution de sa pensée religieuse (1962)
Malraux, Sartre, and Aragon as Political Novelists (1964)
Roger Martin du Gard (1968)
Jean-Paul Sartre (1983)
Jules Roy (1988)
Art as Testimony: The Work of Jules Roy (1989)
An Annotated Bibliography of Criticism on André Gide, 1973-1988 (1990)
Dictionary of Literary Biography, volumes 65, 72, 83, 119, 123, edited (1988-1992)
Simone de Beauvoir Revisited (1991)
Twentieth-Century French Culture, 1900-1975, edited with an introduction (1995)
Retour aux "Nourritures terrestres," edited, with David H. Walker (1997)
Visions of War in France: Fiction, Art, Ideology (1999)
Existential Fiction (2000)
Albert Camus (2000)
Louisiana Creole Literature: A Historical Study (2013)
Southwestern Women Writers and the Vision of Goodness (2016)

Contents

Acknowledgments

The author is grateful to the editors and publishers of the following periodicals and Internet magazines for permission to reprint poems appearing initially there:

Abbeville Review (an Internet magazine): "A Small Poetics," "For the Paris Dead," "On a Postmodern Publisher";

Able Muse: "Dickens at Niagra Falls," "Gloves"; "The Pianist and the Cicada," "Trumpet Vine,"

Chronicles: A Magazine of American Culture: "An Album from Abroad," "Apple," "Bromeliad," "Laura Adams Armer Leaves Her Hogan," "On a Magazine and Its Critic," "Sour Cherries";

First Things: "An Epitaph on My Parents' Graves," "On a Photograph of My Cousin Jean, "Street Piano";

Life and Legends (an Internet magazine): "For a Friend Whose Grandson Killed a Classmate";

Měasŭre: "Flowers on a Train"; two translations from Baudelaire, "The Abyss," "The Voice";

Modern Age: "At Burrough Hill," "Babieca," "Falling," "From the *The Hours of Catherine of Cleves*" (eight poems), "On Taos Plaza," "A Revery";

San Diego Reader: "A Memory of Manaus";

Sewanee Review: "At the Museum Tavern," "Saint-Exupéry over Arras," "Swift and Vanessa," first published in the *Sewanee Review*, vol. 124, no. 3, Summer 2016. Copyright by Catharine Savage Brosman.

A Memory of Manaus

A Memory of Manaus

—For Loren and Janie Slye

We've come by boat upriver some nine hundred miles
along the Amazon, and reached its origins,
the meeting of the Solimões and Negro waters, confluent
but not commingled, flowing for some distance
side by side, in brown and black. This is the very heart
of Amazonia. Sailing upstream, the ship acquired
at the bow a massive trophy—a floating tree, still leafy—
and pushed it into port. We've got three days to tour

on shore. Some travelers have lunch or dine, some shop,
some hire cabs to drive them round the city.
I'm taken one day to a smart resort, with golf course,
fashionable stores, a zoo. Another morning, Loren
gets a cab to hold all four of us. We visit the cathedral,
then the historic opera house, "Teatro Amazonas,"
modeled after those in France and Germany.
The "Rubber Barons" built it, with Palladian façade

and tympanum, and stately dome. In glass cases,
mannequins display the heavy gowns and capes worn
by touring singers in their celebrated roles. The marble,
woodwork, crystal all have been restored, with taste.
To inspect the balconies, I climb the stairs with Loren.
Private boxes draw my eye. Here's the governor's!
Oh my, the man lived well, no doubt, loved well,
maybe. The whole design takes me back to Paris. Pat

cannot do the steps; but later, as a group of visitors
is guided through the hall, he follows them,
admires the ceiling, tests (*sotto voce*) the acoustics,
then breaks out in song —a famous aria from *Rigoletto*.
How appropriate. He gets compliments from tourists;
I am proud. We say goodbye, departing through
the coffee bar. Outside, Janie walks beside him. She
works out; she's muscular. A Proustian moment, then,

almost: Pat stumbles on uneven paving stones. What
he recalls, though, isn't Venice, but his dreadful fall
last year, when someone helping him let go:
deep purple bruises on his side, back, legs, deep pain.—
He sways. I see and hear him; I am steps away.
Before he knows it, Janie has his arm, holding on
for his dear life, and he does not go down; he rights
himself, stabbing with his cane. Perhaps, however,

he was, after all, moved by art and style and happiness—
that glorious nineteenth-century opera in a jungle city,
his thoughts of Verdi and the duke and tragic Gilda,
and his own voice resonating, strong, despite
his weakened heart. We find a taxi to the port;
Pat gets himself on board, lurching a bit. He'll bear
insignia where Janie's fingers left their mark—
tokens of travel, music, friendship, and great age.

Bromeliad

I found it in the trash—a little pot,
discarded thoughtlessly, perhaps in haste.
And yet it's perfect: no dead leaves, no rot—
the poster flower for enormous waste

in everything. Three blossoms—rather, spears—
blood-red and pennate, with enameled sheen,
afford panache that's fit for grenadiers
above a deep rosette of varnished green.

The plant, half-buried, caught my eye, as if
to speak to me. Small miracles occur
discreetly, sometimes shaded, each a glyph
for universals. Why do I prefer

things modest, delicate, and, even more,
the overlooked? They often have a need
which corresponds with mine; I can't ignore
their presence, thinking I should intercede

for them at some vast tribunal of fate.
And they for me? Life dangles by a thread,
precarious; events concatenate,
too—convoluted, devious, instead

of sanely syllogistic, ivy-clad.
The strings get tangled; destinies may clash.
A tufted titmouse, a bromeliad,
and I are fortune's darlings, or her trash.

At the Delachaise Wine Bar

— For Patric, Kate,
and our New Orleans friends

This is my former neighborhood, uptown here
on Saint Charles Avenue, with the streetcars passing
by, ringing their bells (and tourists leaning out
the windows), people running on the neutral ground,
waving their arms, to catch up with the car, sirens,
horns, lots of other noise and hubbub. What a weekend!
It's good to sit a while, just the two of us. I can see,
from our little outdoor table, Touro Infirmary

and the entrance where, months after Katrina,
Guardsmen still were posted day and night, well armed.
My mother died in Touro, long before, her whole body
having given up.— It's late March; the weather's
perfect. We've seen friends at The Columns,
dined on seafood with a pal, met another for some soup,
an affront—not his fault—to New Orleans cuisine,
lunched at the "Grande Isle." And we've spent hours

trying to see a celebrated author whom I know well
but who eludes us every time. Pat wants to meet her,
get her signature for his fine copy (ivory paper,
leather, gilded edges) of her novel. Lots of phone tag:
"Call me after four" and so on. Even here,
at the Delachaise, we hope to hear from her. Meanwhile,
I can eavesdrop on the out-of-towners at the café tables
near us. Strange to belong, yet be, too, an outsider,

that sense of exile which goes back, I gather,
to the garden—the verdant paradise so far behind
us, glimpsed, receding, gone. Well, the famous author
does not telephone. It's late; tomorrow we'll leave
for Thibodaux. Meanwhile, I must forgo
taking Pat to see the Doullut Houses in the Bywater,
built by a steamboat captain, ready to lift anchor (so
to speak) to sail down river, with decks, the pilot house

on top, squared corners, narrow passageways, but also
deep eaves and dipping roof—motifs from "Kinkaku,"
the Japanese house at the great Saint Louis Fair.
Like the autograph, the Bywater must wait.
We order sliders and another glass of wine for me.
Pale yellow tints the sky beyond the river; ships call.
I'm glad I still miss everything—proof of my investment,
which I gave up, for greater earnings of the heart.

False River

—For Olivia Pass,
and for Patric

It's wide, impressive, but it's false—really an oxbow lake,
formed when the Mississippi, on its own, changed
its course, three hundred years ago or so, chopping off a loop,
leaving to the west a "Pointe Coupée"— an "island"
and a flowing *C*. Farther north a bit, there's "Old River"
too, another oxbow, designed by Cap'n Shreve, a shortcut,
practical, for shipping; then, at its other end, "Three Rivers,"
a third detour and a canal linking the great *Meschacébé*

to the Red and Atchafalaya. A pirogue could get lost here,
drifting, ghostly, trapped by river fogs, trees, brambles,
old shacks, derelicts. In contrast, we arrive sanely by way
of St. Francisville, crossing the river on the Audubon Bridge
to New Roads, "Le Chemin Neuf." Listed buildings draw
the eye: a former bank, restored, an old store, the courthouse
(Romanesque revival), and LeJeune Plantation. Oh,
and there's St. Mary's Church, a red-brick neo-Gothic beauty!

The very landscape's old and venerable—Spanish moss,
of course, ancient azaleas, bald cypress, and sixty parish trees
on the Live Oak Registry, with monumental, sculpted trunks
and limbs that graze the ground. But we've no time now
for touring; I've got to speak to the Historical Society,
in their museum, likewise historical. There's chattering
among the crowd, black and white, partly in the local Creole,
maintained by families named Bergeron, Dupré, LeBeau,

Provosty. I am welcomed warmly; aren't we all the children
of the beautiful French tongue? Afterwards, Olivia, Pat,
and I go off for seafood to Morel's, built right on the oxbow,
flanked by camps and docks. Across the water, lights
beam or wink their messages; old street lamps guide our steps
along the gallery, then, after dinner, show us to the bridge.
Why, we ask ourselves the next day over coffee, drive home
via Baton Rouge, the reasonable route? Let's try back roads,

past cattle pastures, fallow fields, the ripening sugar cane,
and bayous edged with waxy myrtle and red oak. Lovely—
but a labyrinth. We wander. One town we hit twice.
I recognize Livonia, where once I ate at Joe's Dreyfus Store,
but that doesn't help. I think now of Three Rivers.
Finally, Maringouin, where, lucky as we are, we find the route
to Lafayette. We've left, though, some of ourselves behind,
the shriving that authenticates paid purchase of experience.

At the Museum Tavern

—London, 2015

I used to come from Sheffield to get warm.
I took the train on Friday afternoon—
a "weekend break"—departing in a storm
or bitter cold, at least. I would cocoon

myself a while in my hotel—a nap,
perhaps—have tea, or get a glass of wine.
Then I'd go walking. No need for a map.
At times the air could be almost benign.

It's still my favorite London neighborhood:
Great Russell Street at Bloomsbury, Coptic Street,
where history, letters, art are understood.
— Again, it's winter; this time, though, there's sleet,

with whipping wind that chills you to the bone.
We went to the Museum first, of course:
sarcophagi and the Rosetta Stone,
Apollo's giant foot, Selene's horse,

the Bassae frieze. They're wonderful, but wore
us out. Since then we've taken tours, half-price
(few others on the bus today—the more
enjoyable thereby), and had a slice

of Englishness; as Dr. Johnson said,
when London's pleasures can no longer hold
a man, he's tired of life, as good as dead.
But now Pat's stiff and weary, and we're cold.

No matter: here's Great Russell Street! The sign
of the Museum Tavern! "Might you stop right here,
dear driver?" Then, as if by some design,
there's an obstruction. "All right, Luv." Oh, cheer!—

light, warmth, an empty table, and a bar
of ancient wood. We're in our element,
preserved together by some prescient star,
both logophiles, with mutual consent,

and still in love, that strange, if worn, conceit—
old actors, barely known, on history's stage,
time's artefacts arranged around our feet
proclaiming the enduring worth of age.

Falling

—Port of Málaga, Spain

Pat could have broken limbs or hit his head
and lost his wits; he could be paralyzed
or have internal bleeding—or be dead.
He's eighty-six; no one would be surprised.

We were to take a tour around the town.
The gangway to the terminal, though steep,
connected high; we had thus to get down.
Where was our tour guide from the ship— asleep?

The escalator beckoned. We'd been told,
Pat says, there was no lift. I hadn't heard.
The terminal could, clearly, not be old.
In vain I looked about; absurd, absurd!

I took the stairs, adjacent; I chose well.
He had more confidence. I heard a scream,
or shout—a noise, I thought, from Breughel's hell,
that terror which can wake you from a dream.

It was, unfortunately, as I feared:
he'd lost his balance, fallen from the top.
He lay there groaning; then the blood appeared.
The awful mechanism wouldn't stop.

The mopping up was done; the doctor came
and wheeled him back. Thank God. We did not lose
much time, nor have a large insurance claim.
A Spanish hospital is not a cruise.

It still was piteous: eight wounds, deep pain,
infection for three months, a grilled-meat scar.
We saw no more, of course, of southern Spain.
At cocktail time, at least, Pat was a star.

This verse is light; the fall was not. He thought
while tumbling, "This may well be *it*." Events
are strange arrangements, where our steps are caught,
and we ourselves but happy accidents.

An Album from Abroad

1. Salt Pans

       —Sailing in the ancient
       Mare nostrum

Málaga, we missed, because, making his way ashore
via the port terminal, Pat fell down an escalator,
precipitous, racing along and slicing skin
and flesh—the awful mechanism finally stopped.
He had to be retrieved, examined, wheeled
back on board, the blood stanched, nicked cane
across his knees. The doctor worked him over,
stitching. So much for sunny Spain, the "eco-friendly

train." Days later, bandaged, hurting, but less shaky,
he is well enough to visit Malta in a tour bus,
waiting directly on the wharf. Risky still, of course.
But prudence is not our sole principle;
we've got hope, with other, companion virtues.
There's something in the air. The guide's a member
of the Order of St. John, a contemporary knight
wearing a tailored suit, the signet of his oath

in his lapel discreet, but eloquent. He's proud
of everything Maltese—churches, the cross,
the Blue Grotto, and a past of seven thousand years—
especially of St. Paul's Bay and, barely emerging
from the modern sea, the islet where, a legend
says, the great apostle landed in a storm,
carried by contrary winds. We drive along the shore,
past fields of artichokes, hand-tilled. I admire

stone fences, groves, a jewel of a chapel, set in time.
Suddenly, on our left, a chain of basins,
shimmering, serene: salt pans—the special labors
of the knights, who work with sun and wind,
the dessication gradual, pan after pan, until the sky
reclaims its water, algae dry, seaweed
crumbles, and the crystals, purified, are fit
for pilgrims, seekers of curiosities, and gourmets—

the salt that we are worth, which must not lose
its savor—salt of the earth, of spirit. —"I have killed
in myself what the beast craved." Shall we too
be panned, becoming crystalline, translucent,
true, refracting sunlight? Shall we, rather, be aspired,
condense, rain gently in the olive trees,
and flow—fluid phenomena, rivers of idea, eddying,
whirling in sea caves, picking up salt once more?

2. In the Souks

—Oman and the Emirates

The souk we visit first, wandering in semi-shadow,
is a covered maze of stalls and shops in Muscat—
authentic, with merchants on their doorstep
hawking goods, or circling like sharks
around their kiosks, black eyes eager, ready pitch,
that enticing smile. "Pure silk." "All cashmere."
"Aladdin's lamp, madame." In the recesses, I think
of Carlsbad Caverns—tunnels, colored lights,

heavy air. Puffs of frankincense assault us.
We make our way through milling men,
broods of children, and madonnas swathed in black
and veiled, as if in shame, denatured. No money
leaves my pocket. Out of the labyrinth at last.
Two days later, passing through Dubai, capital
of Mideast capital, iconic skyline, we reach Sharjah.
Spice shops, proposed, have no appeal; the textiles

must be similar to many others. Now we're driven
to an indoor, air-conditioned souk, a refuge
from the street and worth, to me, a stop, if only
as an anthropologist. We cross the double roadway,
perilous, and discover glitter, riches—Persian rugs,
diamonds, rubies, bracelets, necklaces, tiaras,
wrought in many-carat gold. Again, the women
are dissembled (is their jewelry displayed beneath

those draperies?), except a few bold creatures, upper-
class, of course, heavily made up, and daring to act
westernized. In pairs or threes. They flaunt
their ornaments, their European dress. Pat, taken
by a pressing need, inquires of the guide,
in Muslim garb. "Use the escalator." Heavens, no!
So the fellow, lifting his dishdasha, takes Pat's arm,
leads him to a marble staircase, steep, without

a railing, and gets him there and back, supporting
him. Pat tells me later that the toilet is unspeakable,
a tribal relic, of a piece with trailing robes
and "black disguise." Though cleanliness cannot be
all, it is a start—a freshening of the flesh,
a freeing, so that spirit, even as it needs the body,
is encumbered less. Extremes must touch. What good
is all that gold? Better rather to learn how to live.

3. By the Arabian Sea

—Kochi, India

Now that the local authorities have let us on shore—
three ports, three states, three sets of regulations,
with visa, papers, face-to-face inspection, queues—
we can try again to fathom southwest India,
torn (it and we) between familiarity and something
else—layered and elusive. The traffic, bicycles
and motorized (lorries, taxis, tuk-tuks)—shaving
café parasols, the open stoops of shops, pedestrians—

zig-zags rapidly, dodging almost without pause
any impediment. We make our way by bus
through narrow streets, an avenue or so with trees,
vendors and stalls, trash, and temples—
the ant-hills of men and gods. Past churches also,
since the Portuguese were here, then Dutch, before
the British came. Until his son repatriated
his remains, Vasco da Gama lay beneath the flooring

of St. Francis, a baroque edifice turned Anglican,
with choir stalls, ceilings, tracery, and pews
of dark Victorian wood. Sailing into port, we saw
along the strand the giant curving scaffoldings
for seines of Chinese fishermen, and now,
after the catch, we watch them draw in, hoist,
and stretch the nets for drying. An unplanned treat:
an elephant, tethered beside a temple for a festival,

bejeweled, and munching peacefully on leaves.
The traffic thins; we're nearly in the countryside,
and soon we're on a gravel road, a levee,
raised between flooded fields—not rice, but fisheries,
we're told, with tiger shrimp especially.
Banana fronds and palm trees mark the borders
of the ponds, where birds in numbers feed—
great egrets, cormorants, a gorgeous purple heron,

lesser waders. Suddenly, and then again, the ocean,
silvered through lush greenery—the sea
that brought us here. A heron, elegant, takes wing,
giving motion to the glassy image. All, finally,
is mirror, not window. On another tour,
a woman rode an elephant. Perhaps Ganesha,
trumpeting, will tear the surface of reflection
as we depart this evening. India, farewell, farewell.

4. Missing Mandalay

—Myanmar (Burma)

Another wish not granted us: the old Mulmein Pagoda
and the temple bells of Mandalay. It's just
too far, the trip too rigorous. Pat can endure
a coach tour, but an early flight, a panoramic view,
an overnight, more visits, late return we cannot face.
(The same for Luxor and the Valley of the Kings—
a ten- or twelve-hour day, with lengthy drives
through stretching sands like those of Ozymandias,

then long walks in the heat, descent into cold tombs,
exhaustion.) We'll miss the Irrawaddy River,
Burma's artery, but, after a long and dusty ride
from port, we reach Yankon, at least (to us, *Rangoon*),
via a British-era bridge. Winds play among
the palm trees, sighing, I conceive. Today's a holiday,
honoring General Aung San, the liberator,
and the streets are clogged—small open busses,

cars without number, mostly old, polluting visibly.
Our guide is of good will, but quite obsessed, and led
by her enthusiasm to expound, half-unintelligibly,
on the Buddha, his ideals, the joys of meditation.
"No hate in you; keep serenity." The more
she babbles on, the less serenity. She doesn't mention
war, the Japanese, their victims, nor
a patriot long captive under house arrest. The coach

pulls up to Shwe Dagon Pagoda, monumental, flanked
by smaller ones, like offspring. We can't manage it:
the carpark steps are a deterrent; Pat should not
remove his shoes and socks. The city center is dramatic,
though, thick with commerce, less imposing temples,
and reminders of colonial prestige and elegance.
Churches too—Emmanuel Baptist, appropriately
plain, and Holy Trinity, a neo-Gothic English beauty

built of rose-hued brick, its spire and woodwork
linen white. Beliefs and politics aside, one has a feel
of *laissez-faire* here, mixed with oriental ennui
and charm. "Ship me somewhere east of Suez . . ."
Vague disappointment, too. Since we don't endorse
the New World Order, why not (some wonder)
simply stay at home? Yet this may be, if not Nirvana,
one stage—the test of *caritas*—in our enlightenment.

Apple

According to my gentle Chinese friends,
an apple means serenity; they know.
Here on a *furoshiki,* odds and ends
of Asian origin, arranged for show,

suggest domestic calm: a painted fan,
two lacquered cups, a vase of cloisonné,
a book on bonsai, brought back from Japan
before the war. We'll add to our display

one jeweled apple, polished, brilliant red,
which came from Chinatown, in Singapore,
a present from a shipmate who, instead
of flying home at once, chose to explore

the city, bought this trinket, recognized
my husband on a bench, alone, and thought
to leave with him the souvenir she prized.
We speak of her so often, and she ought

to think of us; she gave us memory,
and also thus enriched herself. The scene—
a parting and an impulse—pleases me.
The apple's hanging by a Chinese screen,

which matches well its green enameled leaf,
gold stem, bright globe. May fortune, which befell
us—minor, but of worth, since time is brief—
wheel round to her now, bearing fruit. Farewell.

Sour Cherries

They charm a painter, birds, and lawless boys
who spy them, steal across the wall, and climb
the trees, denuding limbs. Expected joys
of gluttony turn sour; but petty crime

alone may be rewarding. In a pie,
though—or preserves or compote—fruit and juice,
strained, sweetened, served with spirit, justify
their ruby promise. What we can deduce

from this, for culture, is a moral tale.
Shall Nature be redone, improving taste?
Or should raw spontaneity prevail,
the wild in us that must not go to waste?

The world proposes; we dispose—a stone
becoming altar, vision carved in wood,
a civil pact, inventive epigone
that proves both prudence and ideas of good.

Yet if brute genius seems the better part,
that first, untrammeled devilish desire,
beware of overriding rules and art—
not a refining, but a fateful fire.

Five Translations from Baudelaire

The Abyss

Pascal had his abyss, which moved along
with him. — Desire, dream, act; it all, alas,
is void. I often feel the wind of terror pass;
my hackles rise; fears reach me in a throng.

Around me everywhere—high, low, depth, strand—
cold silence, frightful, captivating space;
and through my hollow nights God leans to trace
an endless nightmare with his practiced hand.

I thus dread sleep the way one fears a hole
agape with horror, vague and bottomless.
Infinity appears through every pane.

Pursued and haunted in my very soul
by vertigo, I envy nothingness.
Ah! numbers, beings, leave me, all insane!

The Romantic Sunset

How beautiful the sun is, rising, new,
like an explosion calling us, complete!
—Most fortunate the ones who then can greet
the sunset, glorious as a dream, and true!

I must remember! I've seen swooning flowers
beneath the sun, an eye, a pulsing heart.
—We must run fast, it's late—yes, yes, let's start
and catch a ray of these expiring hours!

But I pursue the parting god in vain;
night, irresistible, reclaims the plain—
dark, humid, full of shivers, fatal den.

The odor of a mausoleum drifts;
my anxious foot encounters near a fen
toads unforeseen, cold snails, the marsh's gifts.

On Tasso in Prison

— After Eugène Delacroix

The sickly poet in his prison cell,
who rolls his manuscript convulsively,
assesses at a glance his misery,
his spirit's chances in the dizzying well.

Inebrious laughter, echoing, invites
unreason to claim empire in his head;
he's gnawed by doubt; absurdity and dread
in many hideous guises haunt his nights.

This genius shut in misery and fear,
the grimaces, the swarm of ghosts, the streams
of cries about him, whirling at his ear;

this poet, worshipper of the Ideal:
this is your emblem, Soul of obscure dreams,
who choke amid the four walls of the Real.

The Voice

My cradle leaned against a bookcase wall
—dark Babel, holding on its shelves a cache
of novels, farces, fables, science—all
the ancients' lore—Greek dust and Latin ash.
I was no taller than a folio.
Two voices spoke to me. One, pressing, firm,
said, "Life is sweet, a treat, a splendid show.
I can (and then your joys will have no term)
give you an appetite of equal measure."
The other said, "Come travel now by dream
beyond the possible, beyond known treasure!"
That second voice sang like a rushing stream,
a calling ghost, like wind beside the shore,
disturbing, though caressing to the ear.
My wound—a sign—appeared then, bleeding, sore;
fatality had drawn me to its sphere.
Behind existence and its stage, immense,
down in the blackest circle of the pit,
I see strange worlds, distinctly, and their sense—
clairvoyant victim of their benefit—
and drag with me long snakes that strangle breath.
Since then I've loved the desert and the sea;
I've wept at festivals and laughed at death
and bitter wine has brought me ecstasy.
I often take a plain fact for a lie,
and, looking skyward, step into a styx.
The voice consoles me, though: "Dreams must not die,
and wise men's are less fine than lunatics'."

Man and the Sea

Free man, yes, you will always love the sea.
The ocean is your mirror; you see your soul
as breakers infinitely crest and roll;
your mind, a gulf, flows not less bitterly.

You like to dive into that glass; you hold
it by your arms, your eyes; your heart
is charmed from its own murmur as a part
of you to hear that plaint, untamed, wild, bold!

You both are shadowy, discreet, and deep;
for none has plumbed the truths of your dark pools,
O man; none knows, o sea, your wealth, your jewels,
so jealous are you of the lore you keep.

And yet for countless ages you've defied
each other, ruthless brothers, without sense,
both loving greatly death and violence,
eternal strugglers, pitiless, with pride.

Babieca

El Cid had served king Sancho of Castile
till Sancho was assassinated. When
Alfonso—Sancho's brother, heir, and foe—
received perforce the crown, El Cid stayed on,
an honored member of his entourage.
Each was suspicious, though, and rightly so.
The monarch, trying to acquire new lands
among the Taifa city-states and take

Toledo back from Muslim heathen, found
he had been undermined; El Cid had dared
to raid dependencies of his. The king,
irate, prevailed; the great *campeador*
was banished. He was free, at least; he bode
his time as fortune's soldier, serving lords
in Zaragosa—not forgetting, though,
the city on the Tagus and the king,

who bargained craftily with al-Qadir,
its ruler (pressed, besieged by Islamists
from Africa) for safety; in exchange,
Toledo. Legend says that when the king
drew near the city gate, El Cid, behind
him on his steed, named Babieca, passed
a small, unprepossessing mosque. The horse
stopped suddenly and knelt, in awe and prayer;

a holy light, miraculous, appeared.
For underneath the mosque lay vestiges
of what had been a Visigothic church
that Muslims had destroyed. Proof of the grace
of God, perhaps—the Christian warhorse touched,
illuminated, and his rider sure
of his salvation. When Toledo fell
again to Moorish bands, El Cid fought well,

his reputation bright; no help could be refused.
He won Valencia, ruled five years, and died.
His widow took the body, with his horse,
sword, armor, to an abbey in the north,
San Pedro de Cardeña, where the monks
prepared his winding cloth and wove his myth.
For Babieca, on his death, a tomb,
a stele, as for an instrument of faith.

Swift and Vanessa

A Dublin girl, of Dutch extraction, keen
in wit, and beautiful, Vanessa fell
in love at once with Dr. Swift, not yet
the Dean, but eminent and—when he wished—
a magnet. She was young, but not a fool:
one family meeting with him, at an inn,
was quite enough to snare her, willingly.
In London, afterwards, he often dined

with them—and saw Vanessa too, alone;
but fearing spies and gossip, given his place,
they were discreet. The letters they exchanged,
half-coded, half-direct, with pseudonyms,
had many notes on coffee—how they'd like
to meet for "coffee," how her coffee pleased
him ("None worth drinking but your own").—Yet time
was not at his disposal always, filled

by obligations. And there was the friend
called Stella, whom he'd known for years, who may
have been his niece; the rumors even ran
that he had married her, or might. Did Swift
court complication? Did he not know how
to shun disorder? Matrimony seemed,
at least, a risk to happiness. Nor could
two proper English women, even self-

controlled, consent to share a man. When Swift
returned to Ireland as St. Patrick's dean,
Vanessa, then an heiress, followed him.
She settled, with her sister, in a house
outside of Dublin. Talk of "coffee" flew
again. Yet there were shadows on the lawn.
Her letters pleaded with him to be more
attentive, and, perhaps, to marry her—

but futilely. "I'm sure I could have borne
the rack much better than those killing words
of yours." And still he praised her, constantly,
assuring her she was most excellent.
They met sometimes in a bookbinder's shop.
But Stella also was nearby, a threat.
Vanessa, jealous, heard that they had wed;
devoured by doubts, she wrote to ask if such

were true. How Stella must have smiled. "Indeed."
She sent Vanessa's letter on to Swift,
who, caught between them, rode out to confront
its author. Mutely, furiously, he flung
the missive on a table, then stalked out.
Vanessa was consumptive; within weeks
she died. He'd left already for the west—
enduring anger, pain, regret, relief.

Dickens at Niagara Falls

—April 1842
He did not like America—at least
the States—and said so candidly, once back.
Without a notion of proprieties,
uncouth, unlettered, raw: Americans
were not the English. Boston had a bit
of style, though. He had literary friends
through correspondence: Irving, Fields
(the publisher), and then made more. "Boz Balls,"

tours, dinners, meetings—he was lionized.
The lion roared when he presumed to speak
of copyrights and all that he had lost
through ineffective laws; his hosts took note,
embarrassed. Meanwhile, he fell ill from flu,
the weather being nasty and his nerves
well frayed. He kept his schedule, though—New York,
New Haven, Philadelphia. Resolved

to see the South, he left for Baltimore,
where he met Poe. The capital received
him well. But Richmond shocked him—masters, slaves,
too evident, appalling. Next the "west,"
by Pittsburgh, Cincinnati, "beautiful."
Then up "the beastliest river in the world,"
the Mississippi, to St. Louis. Foul—
a ditch—and evil-looking. Floating logs

distressed him; Cairo was "a dismal swamp,"
the soul of ugliness; the river banks
and everything beyond seemed barbarous,
"morasses, bogs," the very settlers wild,
civilization faltering, a threat
to progress, to the gardens of his mind.
So that was nature in America,
a blank, or chaos? He returned by boat

up the Ohio, much relieved, and then
by coach to Cleveland; on to Buffalo,
to see the Falls. A picture for the soul,
at last, the pinnacle of the sublime—
eternity in nature, the Divine.
He hiked down with two British officers
along a slippery bank with melting ice,
still on the U.S. shore, to reach the foot,

then crossed the swollen stream by ferry-boat
to feel the power of the cataracts.
They stunned him into speechlessness—the roar,
the majesty—although he felt strange peace,
beholding his Creator's masterwork.
He stayed ten days on the Canadian side,
admiring the Falls from every point
of view, in sunlight, moonlight, at the edge,

through trees or grottoes in the rocks downstream.
The New World truly might be paradise.
—In darker days, he'd think of molten gold
that flowed at sunset to the crucible
of foam below, of rainbows spanning sky
and chutes, redeeming pain and horridness—
of water poising on the verge as though
to gather strength, and spray of angels' tears.

Charles Dodgson on the Thames

—4 July 1862

Unusually eccentric in an age
of eccentricity, he walked the line,
instinctively, a skilled funambulist,
between proprieties and the abyss
of unconventionality and blame.
Thus Mrs. Liddell saw him as a man
of honor, good at rowing—weren't they all,
at Oxford, then? She frequently allowed

her daughters to step out with him, although
she could turn somewhat cool, or even close
the door a while. Dean Liddell, for his part,
knew Dodgson as a deacon and a don
of Christ Church college. Five of them set out—
the three young girls and Dodgson, with his friend
from Trinity, named Duckworth—for a trip
to Godstow, up the river some few miles.

A fine Victorian scene: a summer day,
smooth lawns and scattered willow tresses draped
above the water, Charles at stroke, the girls,
adept quite early, happy on the oars.
Such outings were not novelties—they'd gone
downstream in June to Nuneham and its park
and gotten drenched, returning home quite late;
they'd often picnicked on the river bank

or played through island afternoons, with tea,
charades, photography. Already Charles
had spun for them long, entertaining tales
of his confection, full of nonsense, wit
(a bit aggressive too), his brain so keen
on logic that he loved its opposite—
the mirror image and the upside-down,
both fanciful and true, revealing more,

perhaps, than might appear to him. That day,
had sleep, or else insomnia, prepared
the plot and the personae in advance?
Or did the Rabbit, Caterpillar, Queen of Hearts,
Mock Turtle and Mad Hatter come to life
full-formed Athenas from the head of Zeus—
enchanting, vaguely frightening? Charles shone,
the characters alive and yet unreal,

the dialogue unmatched. So Alice asked
that all be written down. He marked the date—
a "white stone" in his diary. Underneath
the innocence, however—lacy frocks,
blue ribbons, laughter, friendship, courtesy—
where social niceties did not obtain,
desire seethed, unnamed, for school-age girls,
and Alice most particularly. Sin,

it seems, besotted him the more while she
was near, that summer—nights of agony,
despondent pleas, resolve and prayer. May he
have dared to ask the Dean for her, a child
betrothed, if not a bride? Abruptly, teas
and river parties ended. Five months passed
without a word; the breach was never healed.
Bereft, but clever with his strategies,

Charles met young girls on beaches or through friends,
begged leave to have their company, alone,
took photographs—artistic images,
well posed, some nude. His fame was warranted;
odd whispers, though. Beneath them all, beyond
the century's pale, ran rips of violence
and seismic faults, awaiting time fulfilled,
with sulphurous effluvia and fires.

Bighorn Sheep

—For Clara

They stood, a handsome band, beside the road
to Cripple Creek. "They must be deer," she thought
at first, uncertainly. We had not slowed.
But then she saw the horns, their great curves caught

in sunlight, shell-shaped like a nautilus.
She called out, "Bighorn sheep! Right there! Oh, look!"
—No pull-off, and the drop was dangerous,
with traffic, too; we could not stop. She took

a mental picture for her album: place,
occasion, date. —A bend, a hill, and they
were gone, while the inestimable grace
of girlhood and its images will stay.

Wet Mountains

From Divide, on the north slope of Pike's Peak,
where there's still old snow, the water run-offs split
and turn four ways. As we head south, skirting
the western flanks of the massive mountain fortress,
we leave behind both Fountain Creek, "La Fontaine
qui bouille," and the meanders of the young
South Platte, and pick up a different drainage—
gulches, draws, forks, and creeks, flowing in all

directions—a hand of many fingers, reaching down
along the Arkansas, feeding fruit and vines.
What water everywhere, in this country of dry air!
We follow curves and drop-offs, till we rise
to Cripple Creek and Victor, "City of Mines,"
born from gold, nearly dying once, alive again.
The unpaved side streets boil with dust, but City Hall,
restored, is gilded as in 1900. Here's the address

we want: a small red house, a miner's cabin once,
with added bedrooms, tiny, on one side,
a yellow kitchen (mellow wood; old, stylish fridge),
and a glassed porch, facing east and south, done up
in chintz, mostly blue, and wicker. What sunshine
ripples through, with music—oh, Respighi's suite
"The Birds," lovely! We're treated to a tour.
From a rise—for nothing's level here—we look

to the southwest, past little houses, mine shaft relics,
ancient trees. Far off shimmer the Wet Mountains,
visible in late-summer haze, their famous weight
of snowpack, moisture-rich, implicit still;
and then beyond, the unseen valley, laden now
with new high-meadow hay, and their patron range,
the Sangre de Cristos, half-perceived, half-imagined,
dusty blue—a mantle in a faded painting, aureoled.

Laura Adams Armer Leaves Her Hogan

—Christmas Day, 1936

In '31 her novel earned a prize.
It brought her happiness—an octagon,
traditional: door facing east, dirt floor,
materials from the desert (willows, rock),
built by a Navajo named Klitso. She
had wished for her own Arizona home—
a nomad, having camped on tribal lands
in tents and rented once a one-room house

in New Oraibi to learn Hopi arts
and teach some skills to children in the school
next door. "The desert called, the desert claimed
me," Turquoise-Woman, said, so named by those
who knew her admiration for the stone,
who knew her as an artist. Here she was,
in her own country, but a foreigner,
with Sydney, come from California,

when he was free. He gathered specimens
of cactus for a garden they designed,
then did line-drawings with particulars
(the shapes and sizes, flowers, spines, the scene);
and Laura, who had studied them for years,
composed a text. "It is the poverty
of desert lands that makes life rich," they said.
No flattery was possible, no subterfuge,

just truth. While he was gone, she painted, sketched,
took photographs. The Navajos admired
her (women in particular, to whom
she gave much help), but sometimes grudgingly,
with vague resentment. Later incidents
made trouble. One man asked for money, took
the five she gave him—all she had—but still
in need, went into Gallup, purchased hooch,

intending to resell it, ending up
in jail; his daughter nearly died en route
to free him, through a snowstorm. Laura lived
on borrowed land, on borrowed time. The debt
was called. She organized a feast for all
to mark the Christmastide and celebrate
the sacred turning of the winter sun,
with gifts for everyone. Loud-Talker brought

his newborn babe. And Sydney had arrived;
his present was a quilt, its batting made
from local sheep, with cactus blossoms stitched
in color. In her "lotus-flower house,"
she felt the blessing fallen on them, the fire
of desert comradeship. Farewell. The trail
continues to the Old Age River, bright,
"finished in beauty" and in memories.

Saint-Exupéry over Arras

He'd lived already through four accidents,
none minor: Le Bourget, where Lindbergh found
the world awaiting him; the sea off France
(he nearly drowned); the Libyan desert, past
Benghazi, where his friend Prévost and he—
burnt, starved, dehydrated, and close to death—
were succored by a Bedouin he called "Man,"
the quintessential, nameless rescuer;

and Guatemala, on his way to claim
a prize in Chile. He'd been mobilized
in '39 and wished to fly again
despite his age—not foolish heroism,
but the desire to act for France, to live
by acting. Bodies are an instrument,
a means. Saint-Ex was stationed in the north.
By late May '40 almost all was lost,

the Germans having overrun the east,
the Lowlands, and much else. He was assigned
to do reconnaissance, a futile task,
since what he learned would be of little use.
The roads were clogged with Flanders refugees
and others; Panzers rolled through villages,
and German anti-aircraft ruled the skies.
He flew through flak as in a childhood game

he'd played with others, running in light rain,
attempting to avoid the drops, and earn
thereby a young boy's knighthood. He recalled
long walks in woods—the sheltering trees, soft grass.
"I'm simply strolling, in the evening air."
And he remembered Paula, from Tyrol,
a family governess, who used to put
thick compresses of arnica on sprains

and bruises. "Paula, I shall shortly need
your arnica, quite badly." Flak
continued. How serene the clouds appeared,
how neat and garden-like the earth below,
transformed by motion and perspective—all
concealing mortal danger. He'd become
a tool that went beyond himself, like men
who map the world and stars, or those who tend

the sick, or someone rushing into fire
to save his son.—Saint-Ex's string would not
run out till '44.—Although the plane
was hit and crippled, flying low to take
more photographs, he did not crash, and got
his crew back safely. Exiled in New York,
after France fell, he wrote *The Little Prince*.
"Essential things are hidden for the eyes."

Peggy Pond Church at Los Alamos

When she was just a girl, her father found
the site—another project in the wilds.
He'd tried before to realize his dream
of teaching boys, near Watrous; but it sank:
the Mora River broke its banks, broke lives,
destroying everything. With friends, he next
designed a ranch for dudes from Michigan,
the Pajarito Club. It too collapsed: no rain

(the first year only was quite wet). At last,
on the plateau, he bought Los Alamos,
a ranch, and in '16, began afresh—
a school again, rough living, the outdoors
more useful than the main curriculum
for boys, especially tuberculars,
quite numerous. A new director came
in '17; the family went to live

in Santa Fe, where Peggy went to school.
She was a girl, alas, yet wanted nothing more
than riding, hiking, studying flowers, stones,
collecting shards from ruins. She was sent out
to California for a while, and then
the east, and Smith. She read, she wrote, she missed
New Mexico, its red dust in her mouth,
its famous light, sand underfoot. Then fate

turned up a card for her: a Harvard man
who'd gone out west to teach there, at the school.
They met one summer; he was soon in love.
They wed in '24. She did not love
him; yet she did not care. It was a way
to make her heart's elective place her home,
and change her father's image of what girls
could do. Beginnings for them were not smooth:

she'd not been meant for domesticity;
she was a poet. She had placed some verse
in proper magazines, but distances
were far too great for literary life,
and readers' memories are short. Then, men
and boys require care. They had three sons.
Her life was circumscribed, but thoughtful, thus.
A "poem cabin," built for her alone,

gave privacy for writing; or she'd roam
around the desert. Not quite paradise,
but good enough to lose. "The ripened fields,"
she called those marriage years. The two
survived a crisis of the heart. They camped
and hiked; she traveled some; the boys grew tall.
Imagine then how war would change things, war
that had already done its worst abroad,

in Europe, China, in the islands; now,
the watery Honolulu graves, the war
come home. The famous scientists who cased
the ranch for the Manhattan Project could
not go unrecognized, and rumors flew,
the writing on the wind. When orders came
to close the school, pack up, and leave (except
the seniors, who stayed on through winter term

with their instructors), Peggy took her sons
to Taos. Never would she be again
the girl who thought it hers, Los Alamos,
her heart's desire, her woman's place, a field
of harvest. Trinity came next; she wept
to know a poisoned cloud had burst above
the desert sands, the awful progeny
of what was exile, but had been her joy.

For A Friend
Whose Grandson Killed a Classmate

Her son reported it by telephone:
an argument, a shot. She clutched her throat,
turned dizzy, gave, she said, a sort of moan.
And yet it seemed irreal. She felt remote.

The words, too fixed in memory, resound,
and echo in the papers, in the air.
Few acts, obligingly, go underground
at once; they run and ripple, here and there.

The dead boy's family, grieving, angry, waits
for justice, or revenge. A trial, next;
delays, a verdict, then appeal. The Fates
deliberate. Whatever comes, the text

is suffering.—She *must* be loved by God.
Her father hanged himself, her husband's ill.
So, what is new? The Lord spares not the rod,
nor spoils His child by yielding to its will.

An Epitaph for My Parents' Graves

Their headstones now have sunken into sand,
amid tall weeds, some cholla, scattered sage,
the writing visible, but not at hand.
Their years among the dead compose my age.

That which they did was well done, be it said.
Their journey, both of reason and ideal,
was beautiful, if odd—one step ahead,
one back, advancing in a commonweal

by indirection and the stars. Regret
was rare. They tacked across the desert, found
a pleasant harbor of the mind, and set
their talents and devotion in the ground

like trees. They left again, the port unknown.
Few can appreciate their legacy.
I mark their goodness on the fallen stone
and wave my handkerchief in memory.

Gloves

—In memory of F. K. H.

She suffered in the cold. By Christmastide
each winter, both her hands were cracked and rough,
the knuckles sore. Yet she could not abide
the feel of gloves; the notion was enough

to numb her fingers. Friends' advice, well-meant,
to try another style or size, or let
her bias go, was useless. Someone sent
wool mittens. Wearing them, how can you get

the sense of things, that necessary touch
by which a dexterous hand obeys the eye?
And hers were so well worn, from work and much
devotion. Age alone makes things defy

you, anyway, and gloves would make it worse:
your handkerchief would not come out—instead,
you'd pull the lining; fumbling in your purse
for keys, you'd find a lipstick, a loose thread.

The final years, she rubbed in creams and wrapped
her hands in wispy cloths. It was too late.
She dropped her organ playing. She was trapped,
with fragile skin, arthritic joints, time's weight.

She went out little then, almost alone.
I should have asked her to come south, two weeks
at least, each year. —The winter turned to stone.
Her ashes were dispersed among cold peaks.

At Burrough Hill

—For M. F.

I

From Melton Mowbray south, you drive yourself,
alone, to Burrough on the Hill. You park,
hike up, your mind on visits years before,
your rucksack on your shoulder, holding seeds,
a token. Autumn sunlight, mixed with clouds,
affords fine prospects over Leicestershire.
The hillfort and its great green trapezoid
of Iron Age ditches, ramparts, counterscarp,

its marlstone, varied hues of ores, its ridge
and furrows tracing out medieval fields,
impose millennia of history,
denying time experienced—a day,
a life, a death. But magnifying, too.
That is your purpose: timelessness, or what
comes close to it. Old joys rekindle, quick
and poignant—pools of water on the shore

where memory shines its light; a thought of stars
more brilliant for the darkness, measureless,
that sets them off. —No excavations now;
it's quiet, as if honoring the rite:
his body burnt, new ash, green laurels still.
A shudder seizes you, a chill, or grief;
yet something like a smile redeems the dread
of nothing. —On the Clifton Bridge, which spans

the Avon, son and daughter walk mid-point
to the abyss, a gin-and-tonic each
in hand—his preference—to salute once more
vir probus, father, friend *extraordinaire.*
The moment comes: you cast to east and west
as by a Mesolithic ritual
the hope of flowers and grain; they drink, then toss
their glasses toward the chasm. Hail and farewell.

II

Envoi

To you, a singer, gardener, and muse,
who gather up the emblems of his fame
and evidence of love, by wifely ruse,
arrange his final sheaves, and keep his name,

these lines of homage go, a "tomb,"
a celebration wistful with regret,
averring that, beyond the body's doom,
the music of the mind may echo yet.

Thus Mallarmé remembered Edgar Poe,
"*Lui-même*, forever"; toasted Gautier, well;
and Couperin devised a muse-tableau,
Corelli's master tribute. So Ravel,

to honor Couperin and for a friend
undone in war, composed their double tomb,
exquisitely. Such music has no end,
the Fates reweaving patterns on their loom.

Be consolate; he's left his labors, free,
and rambles in the shadows of a glade,
where letters flourish by Apollo's tree—
conversing, listening, himself a shade.

A Breton Notebook

—For A. R.

1. Market Day

We're guests of Annie in La Trinité-sur-Mer, traveling
by way of Paris and Nantes, deplaning
there three hours late, because in the Paris airport an aide,
come to wheel Pat to a distant gate, separated us,
then abandoned him in a corridor, as I worked my way
alone. Where *was* he?—Found at last—
but with such delay that we missed our connection.
Meanwhile Annie waited in Nantes. What a day! No sleep,

either. —Well, we got here. She showed us her view,
luminous (Place du Voulien, shapely trees, leaves russet,
gold, pale green in autumn sun). She and I
had a glass of wine, and she served a simple meal. To bed,
then, early. She had warned us that today,
below her balcony, the bi-weekly market would begin
at dawn—farmers, fishmongers, *charcutiers*,
bakers, makers of Breton crêpes, all setting up shop

by 6 A.M. No matter; after hearing sounds of vans
and trucks as they pulled up and unfolded
their displays, opening like desks or clam shells, I fell off
to sleep again, rising much later. After coffee
and croissants, she and I go down, shopping bag in hand.
The market's lively, full; no rain.
Here's a vendor of smoked salmon; there's a stall
with fruit and vegetables. Cheeses too, many local,

from black-and-white Breton cows, and meals ready-made
by a nearby chef. All artisanal, if that means
well-selected foodstuffs, hands-on attention
from those who care, and a minimum of handling
and middlemen. We get salad things, Spanish oranges,
apples, a chicken, and for tonight a dish
called *choucroute de la mer*—no seaweed,
as one might fear, and nothing like Alsatian sauerkraut;

rather, a sweeter sort, with scallops, shrimp, pieces of fish.
Delicious. Oh, the French know how to eat!
And perhaps particularly the Bretons, being so close
to the ocean, their cattle and their earth, so close
to tradition—not Parisians, not cosmopolites, jet-
setters, borderless creatures, favoring
"fusion" cuisine—nor foreigners. We toast tomorrow
with *muscadet*—a Nantais wine, fresh, fruity, crisp.

2. Menhirs and Dolmens

This afternoon we drive along the coast,
past megalithic sites. La Trinité
has some; Carnac and villages nearby
have more, with long alignments. Le Ménec
is famous for an army of menhirs
that runs eleven hundred meters, spaced
in rows—almost eleven hundred stones—
quite tall at first, with ample elbow room,

then, sloping, closing ranks, diminishing.
Their stage is time; the drama is unknown.
Remains of circles decorate each end.
Those neolithic Bretons, or pre-Celts, had strength
of limb and spirit! Something in them speaks
to me, deep atavism through my blood.
We visit Kerlescan, Kermario—
more stones in rows—then stop in Plouharnel

to see the burial cairn of Rondossec,
three partly-covered dolmens, well preserved
from some five thousand years ago. Oh, look,
says Annie, in that garden—there!—
a menhir, like an ornament. Just think: glance out
your kitchen window, see memorials
from the distant past, imagine urns and offerings,
and death domesticated, long since with us, still.

3. Concarneau: *La Ville close*

My friends Anne and Patrick have invited us, all
three, for a tour of Concarneau, followed by lunch,
more touring, then return for an overnight
to their house—a historic farmstead from five hundred
years ago, partly restored. We meet them
on the Place Jean-Jaurès, where we can park,
and walk across a short stone causeway to an island
where the walled medieval city—still intact—surrounded

by an ancient moat (filled in), proposes cobblestones,
half-timbered houses, a small city gate opened
to the bay (with a portcullis, for protection
against pirates), ramparts built up by Vauban, residences,
restaurants, and shops with souvenirs. Not vulgar
or ersatz. A church, much younger than the town,
attracts my eye, its baroque lines so different
from the gables and the crooked streets. It's windy,

cool, and with regret, I think of my beret, from which,
in my distress, looking for Pat in the Paris airport,
I somehow got separated. Well, tourist shops can have
their charm: an open door attracts my eye,
and here is headgear, stacked, displayed. Now
I'm well *bereted*, in heavy wool. We pass
the fisheries museum. Oh, at lunchtime I'll have oysters,
flavored with the brine of times past and tradition.

4. Pont-Aven

Gauguin, Émile Bernard, Sérusier
all painted here, among the Aven's mills
and in the fields. Gauguin, before Monet,
did hayricks, sun-washed in the folded hills,

thatched cottages, to show "simplicity,"
a "Yellow Christ," capped peasants, milky clouds—
the "superstitious soul" of Brittany.
The town's still picturesque. Admiring crowds

press down the streets, the river walk. We're due
at Rosmadec, a mill, its waterwheel
still turning, flowers and mossy stones, a view—
and food, we find, of marvelous appeal.

A three-hour lunch, a speciality of France!
We drive down afterwards to Port-Manec'h
and Trévignon. But in the circumstance
we cannot linger; we have quite a trek

to get to Anne and Patrick's at Kerjean.
From their veranda, we look out. The sea!
Again the sea! The last of daylight's gone,
though; night devours our prospect, suddenly.

5: Finistère and Morbihan

We haven't finished Finistère; we five
will visit the interior—*la Bretagne
profonde*. We tour a thatched-roof village, still
in use, then drive through ancient-looking woods
to Saint-Maurice, a ruined abbey, by
the River Laïta, broad, silvery.
White birds fly everywhere. The *crêperie* here
is famous, and with reason. Savory

or sweet, the crêpes are crunchy, buckwheat-brown,
a hundred kinds or more. We say goodbye
to Anne and Patrick, with regret, and turn back
toward le Morbihan and Annie's flat.
What pleasures does she have in store for us
the next few afternoons? An "oyster park,"
called Pô-village; a beach beside Carnac
where one remaining *block-haus* testifies

to Germany's resolve, and madness; Saint-
Cado, an island, where the holy prince
from Wales once disembarked, the legend says,
from a stone trough; then later, Quiberon,
on a peninsula, its western coast
called "savage." And I mustn't overlook
our drive along the Loc'h to Saint-Goustan,
a major fishing port once, now well-known

for picturesqueness (even in the rain,
we liked its granite, watery light, and docks).
We sit outside at a café and drink
hot chocolate; and Annie tells us how
Ben Franklin, sent to France by Washington,
first landed here, en route to ask for help
in Paris. A commemorative plaque
is just too far, though; rain continues. Still,

we are at home with our compatriot.—
Ah, Annie, you have given us the feel
of Brittany, the tastes, aromas, sights,
and sounds—the cool sea air, old stones we trod
on, pearly oyster shells, the smell of crêpes
and fish stalls, cries of circling birds—the past
as it still lives, meaning community
in time, a far dimension of the mind.

For the Paris Dead

—November 2015

The Wehrmacht coveted the wealth of France,
its grain, vines, ports, its past—and Paris most
of all. They planned, and took their shining chance.
Admiring it, they didn't want its ghost,

or ruins! They too were Franks. "Leben wie Gott
in Frankreich" was their watchword. Notre-Dame,
the Eiffel Tower, Concorde, the Louvre, besot
them: vital presence, history, art. The bomb

that struck Saint-Séverin was not a deed
of mad, misogynist fanatics, born
to hate, dehumanized by their own creed,
with Allah's blessing—cruel puppets sworn

to murder or convert.— We see too well
how new attackers want the West to rot;
they'll kill the culture with the infidel.—
It's foolish to be nice. De Gaulle was not,

nor Patton, nor was Charles Martel, who drove
the Saracens from Tours, quite nasty work—
essential, though—nor John, the king who strove
for Christendom, and won, against the Turk.

Past errors stain us, but do not excuse
today's; and suicide remains a crime.
The dead require a stand. Who could refuse?
Requite them, and save France, while there's still time.

Desert

—Northern New Mexico

It's been a wet year—snowfall up through April,
spring rains, and now the budding summer.
Dry washes and arroyos come alive with grass
and rivulets; the dunes and range
have prospered, greening everywhere; yucca
lift their lamps, radiant with milky light, and cholla
blossom like the rose, blood-red. Proprieties
are still respected, though; salt cedar, greasewood,

and mesquite, scattered for efficiency, hold fast
to their small circumscriptions but do not push out
their fellows, leaving space for little cactuses
and low verbena, yellow, purple, pink. Northward,
the Sangre de Cristo mountains raise their summits,
pale, hazy green, tinged—I can conceive—
with violet, the far effect of thick spruce, fir,
and pine. The sky is fully blue. Great outcroppings

of stone repeat the ocher tones of dunes, the glint
of quartz, as sunlight overflows the boulders,
which, like blinded eyes, stare into space, inert;
or otherwise they would have cried out centuries ago,
when Coronado's men left bloody blazes
in the sands and Juan de Oñate cleansed
the pueblo of the Ácoma in punishment, burning,
killing, mutilating, thoroughly. So history,

iniquitous from the beginning, was no better
in the New World than the Old. And, always, just
or unjust, someone pays, at once perhaps
—the avenging angel cometh when he listeth,
assuming countless forms; then, along
the line, others atone, double, triple, twice or thrice.
—We're climbing now, past the cedar mesas,
heading toward high forests, Wheeler Peak,

and Taos. Look—Indian paintbrush, scarlet gilia
among the piñon pine! The Mora River froths,
its currents strong with snow-melt. Time
won't turn around for us; we must do
as the tiniest flowers and microscopic bits of being
in the soil: first endure, in quiet, fearing drought,
the crush of feet; then growing if we can,
respecting boundaries, shunning what is past avail.

On Taos Plaza

We're here to see some friends and get
a dose of culture—chamber music, art
(in painting, jewelry, architecture). Yet
the most important sphere may be the heart.

Two couples, old, one member lame, one ill,
we mark at least the fact that we're alive
at eighty, thereabouts, while love is still
in summertime. And vigor may revive

where we are happiest, among blue spruce
and cottonwoods, and in the famous light
and quintessential air—a fitting truce
of latitude, aridity, and height.

We'll take a slow turn round the square and let
day ripen. Dinner next; and we're not through,
for music waits—piano, string quartet.
Clouds in conceptions illustrate the blue,

and Taos Mountain shimmers in late haze
of turquoise, Maya's necessary veil.
To fortune, then, long love, new health, we raise
a toast—along the Old Age River trail.

Blue River

From the heights of Hoosier Pass, it flows northward—
trickles in the soil at first, next a brook,
then a stream, still small but bouncing over stones,
and finally white water, meeting at Kremmling
the Colorado River. Most of the way,
we have fir and Engleman spruce, blue spruce also,
lots of aspen, as well as undergrowth.
We've got a little picnic lunch, but nowhere

to lay out our spread and sit. Finally, we choose
a turn-off used by fishermen. Plenty of place
to park, at least. I get the hamper, cooler,
and my hat, and soon we're seated under aspen,
each on a rock, close, however, to the precipice
that leans down to the river. Oh, these rocks are hard,
and hardly bearable. We munch on ham and cheese
and fruit; Pat drinks some milk. Time, then,

to get up. He can't: the rock is low, the ground
slants off behind him. I pull; he lifts himself a bit,
but loses strength and totters back, quite near
loose soil, and then falls flat. Two bikers
at the other end, admiring the view, look good enough
to me; I run to get them, and they come,
of course, a couple, sturdy each, and kind. We thank
them warmly as they help Pat to the car,

unsteady, grateful. On our way then. It's late August;
touches of pale yellow in the trees,
like last glints of daylight, speak of fall. The slopes
are almost bare of montane species here,
and soon it's sagebrush, over brown terrain, for miles—
and, too, many miles of road construction,
along with conservation projects—high fences
so the elk will not keep running on the road. Well,

it's their territory. Yet we don't see a single animal—
not with such commotion. The river has run
with us—well below and lost among the willows,
or at our level, visible—and now we cross
it, separating. In Routt County, to the northwest,
good friends await us, food, drink, cheer;
but leaving the Blue River is leaving the living flow
of summer, that felt music which you cannot hold.

On a Magazine and Its Critic

It claims to be a high-class rag,
and dictate literary taste.
The critic's photo made me gag,
his contents nasty, worse than waste.

His xenophilia comes out
as he surveys the current scene.
Unreconstructed fools, don't doubt
your preferences are unclean.

Pontificating in his fanon,
he summarizes what he sees.
Good heavens! Reference to the canon,
tradition, measure—enemies!

Those ancients were abusive, cruel,
slave-owners, sexist, racist too,
Their myths are false, the thinnest gruel;
their "wisdom" would not fill a shoe.

The Renaissance, another crime,
pretentious, born of church and court,
should be discarded for all time;
we can't afford such classist sport.

Envoi

He wants to banish dead white men.
Won't he be one? Alas, what then?

A Small Poetics

A poetess, invited to submit
her verse—a friendly offer— answered back:
"Your editorial policies don't fit
my own advanced ideas; I'd be a hack

if I were to contribute. Life is short,
and poems few; I want them to do good,
and advertise my causes." That retort
astonished me. So poems, briefly, should

be activist endeavors, meant to serve
some special interest? I cannot believe
Erato and Polymnia deserve
demotion thus, or that they can achieve

their own fulfillment in a servile role
promoting "progress." Poetry is art
and not reform; it is the very soul
of life and thought, their lasting counterpart.

Envoi

Tradition—that's the unforgiven sin.
Why did I ever think to ask her in?

On a Postmodern Publisher

A modest query falls out of the fog:
"Might you be interested in this small book,
which would appear to fit your catalogue—
new figures, new research? Please take a look."

The answer is politely couched, and smooth;
they cannot risk offense that might be quoted.
The momentary business is to soothe,
while the assessment's "pending, as was noted."

They read the work in-house, then send it out
for two evaluations, with a letter
that may be poison-pen. It's all a rout:
the first review is bad, the next no better.

"You have no overarching argument.
Now, Hegel organized all history,
a pyramid of theses; Marx then went
a step beyond, and found economy

to be its moving force. Edward Said
produced his post-colonial critique,
and feminists imposed their brilliant creed:
collective guilt; no grace. Oh, *magnifique!*

—>

So what's your thesis; what's the guiding claim
in this poor manuscript? One must devise
a pattern, make things fit, not simply aim
at facts or themes, a pedant's enterprise!

You see, a book must *do*, and not just *be*
or be *about*. This study will not stand
unless you can construct some theory,
invent a meaning—even find a *brand*."

The shelves groan now with useless stuff unread
and quite unreadable—tendentious, dense,
absurd. Since, in the long run, we'll be dead,
why give our time to things that make no sense?

Envoi

Postmodernism is a dreadful farce.
Why don't they go and stuff it up their.....?

In the Whitney Museum

So, Donald Judd said, "If you think it's art, it is."
What if you think it *isn't*? The Whitney, we are told,
has signs at some exhibits saying "This is art!"
People used to *know*—to recognize at once
a bench, an air duct, or the toilet cleaner and her trash
as practical accessories and not displays. Artists drew,
sculpted, painted, made subjects moving, beautiful—
having at least aesthetic truth, a bit of the sublime

or *je ne sais quoi*. Think of Michelangelo, Velásquez,
of "The Raft of the Medusa," or Prendergast, right here.
Even the moderns: in Picasso—like him or not—
you can identify the noses. In avant-garde galleries,
while they don't dare preach against elitism,
the upper class, or money (where would they be without
it?), they cultivate what most offends us and contrive
to make us feel philistine. —*À la rigueur*, I'll take

a vein of the grotesque; the vile is too much. They
did not invent it anyhow. —There's more, however.
The Whitney *politburo* broke into a wall
in its new quarters, to entomb a strange *objet d'art*.
It's just as well we didn't see it first— not
possible, since it was encased inside a concrete block;
and furthermore, the *objet* was destroyed nine years
ago by steamroller—part of the sculptor's plan,

one Cattelan; so it's *remains*, or *dust*. (It showed him
seated at a table, dining on spaghetti, face plunging
in the plate. How elegant.) Then, the homicide—
orchestrated crushing, burial in the old building,
disinterment, and concealment in the new, the Press
invited in. The public did not see the burial rite,
though; only the initiated. Skeptics don't believe
the thing existed. Abstract art indeed! The hierophants

assure us it is there; but that is how Egyptian priests
deceived the masses and their sycophants,
with ritual, rich vestments, arcane lore, and claims
of power behind the veil. What's the unseen worth?
It's reputation only. —But Cattelan can laugh
at criticism; at Sotheby's, a work of his fetched almost
eight million dollars. "Destroy, destroy," pronounce
the newest gods! And ceremoniously, not by war or fire

(as if *they* weren't enough). Let's all commit, pistol
to our temples, cultural suicide, stroking our egos
meanwhile, expressing our complexes, and admiring
masterpieces such as Cattelan's ersatz pigeons
and their feces, shown in Venice. "Ruu ... bbish!"
as a man from Yorkshire shouted at some modern music.—
You have to know how far to go too far. But we've
got world enough and time, until it all runs out.

A Revery

We're in a private garden—Arcady.
Cool windmill palms, Cape jasmine, climbing rose,
live oaks, a fig, the archetype of tree,
magnificent magnolias: all propose

light, leafy thought, while scattered notes of dread
and pain, remembered, barely interfere
as being spins unceasingly its thread
out of our substance and the atmosphere.

What artistry is on display!—through chance,
intentions, Nature's talent, which contrive
to model the ideal from circumstance,
the lost originals that still survive.

Contentment, calm, are not mirage. To be
in sentimental misery (intense,
grotesque, or bitter) antithetically
presumes acquaintance with a garden's sense.

Such dialectic shapes the afternoon—
aromas, murmurs lingering in the grass,
moist air, fresh late-spring breezes, opportune;
yet stillness, even as the moments pass.

We have been happy, you and I! These hours,
a benefit of friendship, time, and love,
hang trellised, framed in foliage and flowers—
the meaning in the manner, hand in glove.

Street Piano

— For P. A. Michels

The movers get it out—a Steinway grand,
half-rolled, half-carried to the street. A crowd,
molecular, implicit, is at hand
already. Music hovers meanwhile, proud

to weave into the day an ideal strand.
The pianist appears, hirsute and browed
like Rubinstein. Who would not understand
this may be *Art*? He pauses, turns. A loud

commotion follows. Noise? No, it's a chord
by Beethoven that crashes on our ears.
Attention, everyone! Those who are bored

may leave. The rest are lifted to the spheres
as flights of sound riff on, a rippling stream.
The city is, for now, an angel's dream.

On a Photograph of My Cousin Jean

As lovely as a girl aged twenty-two
can be—intelligent, slim, self-possessed,
and beautiful. It's Florida; it's new
to her, like marriage. Smiling, smartly dressed,

she poses, shaded by a palm, beside
a terra cotta jar. The honeymoon
has just begun, the cattleya fresh, the bride
still radiant. Life, though, finds her out too soon,

a willing instrument. And now the horn
of age has sounded, with a mellow tone,
yet wistfulness; her handsome heart is worn,
and on her sleeve—why not?—since she's alone.

Time, thrifty, used her well, as she allowed;
and she gave back, by plan, by circumstance,
from mind and body both, and richly—proud
to live the meeting of intent and chance.

Flowers on a Train

They met at Euston Station for their last
farewell, the coda to a London tryst.
"Goodbye, goodbye!" The moment came, and passed.
She lingered, found her quay, but almost missed

the train when he returned with a bouquet
bought hastily next door: exquisite blooms,
white roses, iris, daffodils, a spray
of baby's breath, the thought of many rooms.

He pressed them on her in a quick embrace.
In tears, she ran, climbed up, and got a seat.
She held the flowers like a bride, her face
more radiant in despair, the break complete.

Eye

That huge cow eye, surgically extracted out of head
and socket, looked at me nonetheless, from its dish
on the laboratory table. I felt faint, clammy, cold;
as the French put it, fittingly, "J'ai tourné de l'oeil"—
or *something* in me turned, at least—the stomach,
chiefly. Embodiment too evident, a faculty reduced
to its instrument? Or general Sartrean disgust at flesh—
the deep revulsion of consciousness demanding to be

pure reason, when nature has instead enveloped it—
fashioned it—in viscous, involuted, slug-like tissues?
My cranium, a vessel (think of Hamlet and of Yorick's
skull—oh, *Vanitas*), holds mind, which holds the idea
of mind; thus my mind contains my mind.— What
an organ is the eye!—what greedy grasp, not satisfied
with objectives close by (on clear days, you can see
the San Juan Mountains from the Great Sand Dunes,

one hundred miles away). Thus that cow eye, glaucous,
vaguely like a skinless grape, yet still alive (to me)
and staring at me as I took it in (too empathetically),
though deprived of function and ungrounded, was as
my own, the image (one may truly say) of man seizing
the world, which may escape our hands, our praxis—
but yields to vision. —More or less. If appearance
may well be the very thing, *Dasein*, its color, contours,

texture, size, what of its hidden sides—that aspectual
resistance, half a lamp, the dark side of the moon? And
the eye barely grazes things, glides past, a wind leaving
little trace. Can I touch that mountain as I draw it near,
feel the shade, or enjoy the sweet aroma of gardenias
in the florist's window? And how is it that two lines,
narrowing, rising skyward, thinning, gone, really are
the road? Enough! The Great Orb of Day, all morning

well concealed, finally has raised its cloudy lid to gaze
at us. Zeal, zeal! A thought, ethereal but eidetic, comes
of its own will; my inner eye enfolds the circumference,
then fixes on a field of scarlet Indian paintbrush, mixed
with the deep cerulean of bluebonnets, illuminated
and illuminating—then on the watery silver of Monet's
lily pond, below the bridge, thick with iris, shaded over
by a pensive weeping willow, greened with lilies of idea.

Trumpet Vine

Chromatic fanfares in the garden flash—
nasturtiums, dahlias, phlox, blue columbine—
around the feet of pine and mountain ash,
antiphonally with a trumpet vine,

which, by its adventitious rootage, climbs,
displaying pennate leafage: emerald green
when new, then later dark; vermillion cymes
with yellow throats articulate the scene.

It's *campsis radicans,* though; suckers spread
and propagate their kind with greedy ease;
thus woody growth, unpruned, can get ahead
of us and strangle hospitable trees.

No matter now; that garden is a ghost—
a vital plant become a paradigm
of death; perennials gone; a fallen host;
the horticulturist choked off by time.

Philosophy does not suffice; one needs
fresh laughter, mountain air, the scent of pine
and flowers of remembrance, even weeds,
to match the high notes of the trumpet vine.

The Pianist and the Cicada

—Aix-en-Provence, circa 1962

The cloistered court of the archbishopric
is full. It's summer. The piano's there.
There's stirring, expectation; dusk is thick
with garden sounds. Then Rubinstein, his flair

upon his sleeve, arrives. First, Chopin, Brahms,
both very brief. He wipes his beading face.
More Chopin. A cicada in the palms
begins to sing—a southern commonplace.

The master shapes the phrases: tender—tense—
expressive. Through the notes, however, comes
the insect's steady song. The audience
grows nervous, hearing their duet: one hums

insistently; the other strokes the keys,
hot-tempered, though. He could ignore a cough
or shuffling feet; not mating calls from trees.
He was about to start Rachmaninoff.

He pauses; the cicada pauses, too,
but sings again when he begins to play.
The prelude falls apart—a Waterloo.
He rises, bangs the lid, and strides away.

There is no refund; nature does not care,
nor management, it seems, nor Rubinstein
the least of all. We can't be unaware
we're often nothing in the grand design.

From *The Hours of Catherine of Cleves*

(Suffrages)

1. Conversion of Saint Hubert

Astride a handsome dove-grey, long-limbed horse,
a rider richly capped and dressed with art
stops suddenly, arrested in his course,
bewildered by a wondrous rearing hart.

The reins are stretched and taut; the steed pulls back.
The holy stag, its forelegs crossed, displays
a crucifix encircled in its rack.
A hunting dog, its paws together, prays.

The halo is already done, its gold
contrasting with the hunter's smart attire.
The future and the past, the new, the old
to Christ are all one moment—spark, flame, fire.

2. Martyrdom of Saint Erasmus

Imagination led to the machine—
a spindle in a frame, above a bed
on trestles, where, unnaturally serene,
Erasmus lies, well bound, with mitred head.

The executioners each turn a wheel
to wind, from where his stomach is incised,
the saint's intestines. There is no appeal;
though one man leans away, the death is prized.

The landscape, verdigris and bare, is low;
the sky, of white-tinged blue, betrays no grief;
no mourners pictured in the border, though
a hobbyhorse and child give strange relief.

3. Saint Agatha

With pincers, she displays a severed breast,
her attribute. There's some distaste, but pride—
the womanly adornment cruelly wrest
has marked her as a most unlikely bride,

save to her Lord. The background emblem, red
and gold—a phoenix rising from his ash,
the spirit's figure, toward her radiant head—
provides a feathered, marvelous panache.

Her dress hangs straight; she lets her mantle fall,
not seeking, obviously, to conceal
the mutilation. Jewel motifs recall
her patronage of smiths, the fire's seal.

4. Saint Ambrose

Attired in green surplice and a cope,
the bishop holds his crozier and a book,
insignia of sacrifice and hope.
He's bearded, though not ancient, with the look

of charity. The legend underneath
reads "Pontifex." A puzzling design
around the portrait draws the eye: a wreath
or necklace made of mussels—not his sign.

A mystery. The shells are drawn with care,
the outside dark and rayed, the inner pearled;
a crab provides a clasp. That they must bear
our appetites bespeaks a fallen world.

5. Saint Martin Dividing His Cloak with a Beggar

The soldier, mounted, turning sideways, holds
his sword, unsheathed. The beggar, with a crutch
and wooden leg, already has the folds
of half the mantle on his shoulders. Such

seems groundless; why not give the other part?—
The soldier owned but half. The Amiens gate
at sunset is as crimson as a heart.
For *agape*, it cannot be too late.

A second crippled beggar lifts his bowl.
Above, Christ shows the cloak, like that he set
aside at Calvary; a banderole—
a winding sheet—unfurls, the lasting debt.

6. Saint Catherine

A patroness for Catherine of Cleves,
the holy woman stands among the signs
of martyrdom. Around the portrait, leaves
of varied colors, with fantastic lines.

Beside her, adumbrations of her pain
to come—a dwarfish man with wheel and sword.
She holds a book; her interest does not wane.
She waits upon the wisdom of the Lord.

Did Catherine of Cleves believe that all
was sanctified—grief, error, levity?
Among the leaves, a bear cub throws a ball;
so *felix culpa* bought salvation's tree.

7. Saint James Minor

The saint—well clad in garb of red and brown,
and holding beads, a curving pedum staff—
though less than Great, is not without renown.
The master artist knows it; he can laugh.

For James was famous for his abstinence;
yet even Jesus blessed the wedding wine
at Cana and the chalice. No doubt whence
the motives at the foot: a stylized vine,

an empty tankard, and an outdoor stand
where someone fills a pitcher from a cask.
A sculpted angel smiles in Rheims; at hand,
to taste God's vintage is a joyous task.

8. Saint Christopher Carrying
   the Infant Christ

It's richly drawn, a multi-action scene.
The Infant, on his shoulder, holds a globe
and blesses Christopher, whose mantle, green,
drags underfoot; his cut-off scarlet robe

may be in tatters. At the lower edge,
the gates of Gaza fall, a parallel.
The saint is weary. On a rocky ledge,
a hermit lifts a lantern; wavelets swell.

As orange sunset fades before the night,
the saint leans on his staff, as if he bore
a growing stone. The moon is high, to light
the shallows, and the bearer steps ashore.

Endnotes

"At the Delachaise Wine Bar." The term "verdant paradise" is a reminder of Charles Baudelaire's phrase "Le vert paradis des amours enfantines" (The green paradise of childhood loves).

"An Album from Abroad."

"Salt Pans." The quotation in the last stanza comes from André Malraux, commenting on a passage from *Terre des hommes* (*Wind, Sand, and Stars*) by Antoine de Saint-Exupéry.

"In the Souks." The phrase "black disguise" was used for the *abeyya* by Lady Mary Wortley Montagu, the eighteenth-century letter-writer, who lived in Turkey for six years.

"On the Arabian Sea." In Hinduism, Ganesha, the son of Shiva, is the elephant-headed god.

"Missing Mandalay." The phrase "Ship me somewhere . . ." is, with the Mulmein Pagoda, a reminder of Rudyard Kipling's "The Road to Mandalay."

"Apple." For the Chinese, traditionally, the apple is a symbol of peace, the peach, one of long life.

Translations from Baudelaire. Except for "Man and the Sea," from *Les Fleurs du mal* (1857), these poems are from *Les Épaves* and *Les Nouvelles Fleurs du mal* (both published in 1866, although certain poems or portions thereof may have been drafted earlier). Baudelaire's sonnet form allows for various rhyme arrangements.

"Babieca." This poem traces briefly important episodes in the career of El Cid (Rodrigo Díaz de Vivar), including transfer of his body by his widow from Valencia, which took place three years after his death. The historic fact is that when Alfonso VI of Castile entered Toledo, whose acquisition he had carefully planned and carried out, in 1085, El Cid was not with him; he remained in exile until late 1086. But legends, multiplying around him, placed him with the king. The present one, involving Babieca, is based on a version told by Gustavo Adolfo Bécquer, a nineteenth-century Spanish author.

"Swift and Vanessa." Information on Swift and Vanessa (Esther Vanhomrigh, d. 1723) and the quoted phrases come from *Jonathan Swift, His Life, His World*, by Leo Damrosch (2013). As Damrosch and earlier biographers concede, much about Swift is speculative, and clues are interpreted variously. That Swift married Stella (Esther Johnson) in 1716 or at another date has been neither proven nor disproven, nor is his parentage certain, nor hers; thus their blood relationship is unsure. The encounter between Vanessa and Swift, after Vanessa wrote, purportedly, to Stella to inquire about the putative marriage, is recounted by Thomas Sheridan the younger but cannot be corroborated.

"Dickens at Niagara Falls." The data and quotations come from Charles Dickens, *American Notes for General Circulation* (1842).

"Charles Dodgson on the Thames." Details on the July rowing expedition and speculations recorded here are borrowed from the sympathetic and judicious study by Morton N. Cohen, *Lewis Carroll: A Biography* (New York: Knopf, 1995). In the immediate Oxford area, the Thames was then called the Isis, as it still is often, but since the letters of that name have become a political acronym associated with Islamic militancy and hatred, it is not used here.

"Laura Adams Armer Leaves Her Hogan." Details come from essays in her *Southwest* (1935), *The Trader's Children* (1937)—a fictionalized version of her experience—and her memoir *In Navajo Land* (1962). Her phrasing is borrowed for certain lines here in addition to the quotations. Sydney, a renowned commercial artist, was her husband. The prize mentioned is the Newbery, awarded for *Waterless Mountain*; she won others. Armer, who used the term, surely knew that the Navajos called the San Juan "The Old Age River." (This phrase reappears in another poem of this collection.) After 1936, she and Sydney lived in California. She died in 1963 at the age of 89. The phrase "Finished in beauty" and its variants are common throughout Navajo chants and ceremonies, and are used by other peoples and by twentieth-century writers.

"Saint-Exupéry over Arras." Information and some of the phrasing here come from Antoine de Saint-Exupéry's *Pilote de guerre* (*Flight over*

Arras), published in English and French in 1942 (circulated underground in France). In 1943 he left New York for North Africa, where he was able, despite certain obstacles, to rejoin his air squadron and, with special permission, fly reconnaissance missions. (He was deemed too old and too unwell for combat flights.) He disappeared in July 1944 on a flight over the Mediterranean. In 2000 portions of his plane were found underwater; they were identified positively in 2004. Why he crashed or who shot him down has not been determined; claims are contradictory.

"Peggy Pond Church at Los Alamos." Ashley Pond, Jr., the son of a Detroit industrialist, was sickly as a boy. Dropping out of Yale, he joined Theodore Roosevelt's Rough Riders but fell ill of typhoid and was unable to see action. Recovered, he headed for New Mexico, met Peggy's mother, of pioneer stock, married, and launched the ventures sketched here. Though Peggy (1903-1986) published work in the *Atlantic Monthly* and *Poetry*, her books and chapbooks appeared mostly locally. Through a friend, Edith Warner, she knew J. Robert Oppenheimer. She and her husband, Fermor, never returned to Los Alamos to live, though they did settle later in Santa Fe. Although the Antiquities Act of 1906 forbade mishandling of ancient artifacts and potsherds and removal except by authorities, gathering of potsherds was widely practiced in the early decades of the twentieth century, both by those wishing to resell them and by locals collecting for themselves. Around 1919, the potter of San Ildefonso, María Martínez, and her husband created their famous ware on the basis of an unusual shard they found in nearby ruins.

"For the Paris Dead." Ernst Jünger (1895-1998), the author of *Storm of Steel*, who served as a staff officer in occupied Paris, epitomized the admiring envy Germans had long felt for France. The Wehrmacht did not carry out wholesale destruction in Paris, despite an earlier declaration by Hitler, repeated shortly before the Liberation (August 1944), that if retreat became inevitable the city should be razed. Bombs had been placed at strategic positions, and "maximum damage" had been ordered. Various figures contrived to have the orders contravened, generally. Nevertheless, the presence of Resistance elements as well as other circumstances contributed to street fighting and damage. The apse of the Church of St. Séverin, on the Left Bank, was hit. (It was beautifully rebuilt.) Cultural destruction is a major goal of Islamists. It will be recalled that hijacking bombers of September 2001 were to blow up the Capitol in Washington. One thinks also of the Buddhas of Bamiyan in Afghanistan and similar statues in Pakistan destroyed, at great pains, by the Taliban.

"In the Whitney Museum." The sculptor is Maurizio Cattelan, an Italian. His proclaimed attitude toward art parallels somewhat that of the pseudonymous Banksy, with his slogan, "It's not art unless it has the potential to be a disaster." The last lines here are approximate quotations from Jean Cocteau and from Andrew Marvell's "To His Coy Mistress." See the *New Yorker*, 4 May 2015, for information on the transfer of the "remains" to the new building. It should be understood that the present author is under no illusions that the poem will lead to artistic reform.

"Trumpet Vine." The flora mentioned are suited to most latitudes and elevations in Colorado, from Denver and Colorado Springs to Bailey, Woodland Park, and higher.

"The Pianist and the Cicada." Arthur Rubinstein performed at the Festival International d'Art Lyrique in Aix-en-Provence circa 1962. The incident related is true.

"From *The Hours of Catherine of Cleves.*" This ekphrastic sequence refers to the published volume, with introduction and commentaries by John Plummer (New York: George Braziller, n.d.), the two-part manuscript of which (now in the J. Pierpont Morgan Library) dates from about 1440 or slightly earlier and was produced in Utrecht for the eponym, perhaps when she became Duchess of Guelders. The poems bear the titles assigned to the illuminations, which, when featuring one or two saints (as opposed to scenes from the life of Christ and other biblical tableaux, usually multi-figure), are called *suffrages*. It should be noted that *panache* here has its first meaning: a tuft of feathers used ornamentally. The Smiling Angel of Rheims dates from 1236-45. It is sometimes identified as the first smile in medieval ecclesiastical art.